"Brian Albert is a skilled and caring shepherd of souls. His *Living the Faith* is a trustworthy, biblically-sound resource for discipling a new believer. It is practical, easy to understand, and contains dozens of thought-provoking questions for private consideration or meaningful dialogue."

Donald S. Whitney
Professor of Biblical Spirituality and Associate Dean
The Southern Baptist Theological Seminary, Louisville, KY
Author of *Spiritual Disciplines for the Christian Life* and *Praying the Bible*

"One of the key aspects of the Christian life is discipleship. And discipleship requires personal piety. And personal piety is fed by devotion. And devotion is aided by this little book by Brian Albert. Many Christians neglect their personal time with God and this volume is a wonderful aid to restoring that time with God to a place of importance. Wise, helpful, and filled with spiritual truth, Brian's book will help you to re-establish, or establish for the first time, a devotional life worthy of the name."

Jim West
Lecturer in Biblical and Reformation Studies
Ming Hua Theological College
Author of *The Person in the Pew* Commentary Series

Ministry and Discipleship Guides

Grounded in the Faith: A Guide for New Disciples Based on the Apostles' Creed, by Todd A. Scacewater
Internalizing the Faith: A Pilgrim's Catechism, by J. Brandon Burks
Living the Faith: Upward, Inward, Outward, and Onward, by Brian Albert

Living the Faith

Upward, Inward, Outward, and Onward

Living *the* Faith

Upward, Inward, Outward, and Onward

BRIAN ALBERT

Fontes Press

Living the Faith:
Upward, Inward, Outward, and Onward

Copyright © 2019 by Brian Albert

ISBN-13: 978-1-948048-07-1

Scripture quotations are from the ESV® Bible (The Holy Bible, English Standard Version®), copyright © 2001 by Crossway, a publishing ministry of Good News Publishers. Used by permission. All rights reserved.

All rights reserved. No part of this publication may be reproduced, stored in a retrieval system, or transmitted in any form or by any means—electronic, mechanical, photocopy, recording, or any other—except for brief quotations in printed reviews, without the prior permission of the publisher.

Fontes Press
DALLAS, TX

www.fontespress.com

To Anita, without whom...

Contents

	Preface	xi
	Introduction: The One Thing	1
1	Upward Spirituality	9
2	Inward Spirituality	21
3	Outward Spirituality	31
4	Onward Spirituality	39
	Conclusion	51

Preface

The aim of this work is to provide followers of Jesus with a basic understanding of Christian spirituality in which to disciple new believers. I would like to thank Todd Scacewater and the entire staff at Fontes Press for providing me the opportunity to contribute to this series. Many thanks should be granted to Trey Dimsdale for making the connection. I am indebted to my church family, Calvary Baptist Church of Lenexa, Kansas for the fifteen years to serve as your pastor. Lastly, to my family, Anita, Emma, and Noah, who make every day a joy.

Introduction

The One Thing

Wilson Bentley was known as the "Snowflake Man." Born and raised in a farming town of Jericho, Vermont, he was thrilled to venture outside during snowstorms. For his fifteenth birthday, he received a microscope, which he used to examine snowflakes. By age nineteen, he constructed a crude camera that was able to take photographs of these snow crystals. Eventually, he turned his findings over to scientists who scoffed him away when he suggested that no two snowflakes are alike.

But this rejection did not deter him from pursuing his passion. Bentley's fascination for snowflakes led him to record detailed weather observations. Eventually, he filled nine books with 47 years of notes about snow, frost, dew, and rain. During his lifetime, Bentley's work was largely ignored, but after his death his data became pivotal information on daily weather conditions some of which are still used by the National Weather Service. He died at the age of 66 after catching pneumonia while walking home in a blizzard.[1]

What makes a man live and die for snowflakes? One word: passion. Bentley testified, "I wouldn't trade places with Henry Ford or John Rockefeller for all their millions! And I wouldn't change places with a king: not for all his power and glory. I have my snowflakes!"[2] His life was consumed with this drive, and he did not care if people thought him odd, or if he was poor, or if the science community scoffed at his works. He loved snowflakes and, curiously, died fulfilling this passion.

King David reigned during the "Golden Age" of Israel. His journey from shepherd boy to ruling

---

[1] For more information about Bentley see, Duncan Blanchard, *The Snowflake Man* (McDonald & Woodward Co., 1998).

[2] Pam Wilson, *Falling Into My Place* (Westbow Press, 2015), 25.

monarch has been retold through the ages. Scripture describes him as a "man after God's own heart" (1 Samuel 13:14). But how does Scripture articulate David's passion? We discover it when he confessed, "One thing I have desired of the Lord, that I will seek after; that I may dwell in the house of the Lord all the days of my life, to behold the beauty of the Lord, and to meditate in his temple" (Psalm 27:4). David desired *one* thing...to dwell in God's house...to behold God's beauty...to meditate in God's temple.

Mary and Martha were sisters who hosted Jesus and his disciples. During one particular visit, Martha was busy with tasks around the house and she rebuked Jesus, because he had not rebuked Mary for failing to help her serve (Luke 10:39). "Tell her to help me. Don't you care?" Jesus' response was instructive. "Martha, Martha, you are anxious and troubled about many things, but one thing is necessary. Mary has chosen the good portion, which will not be taken away from her" (Luke 10:42). We learn that Mary was sitting at Jesus' feet, listening to Him (one thing), while Martha was busy about much service (many things).

Prior to his conversion, the Apostle Paul had "outstripped his contemporaries" in law keeping.

He listed his credentials more than once. In religious self-righteousness, Paul was the G.O.A.T. (Greatest of All Time). Yet he called these accomplishments rubbish, garbage, and trash. He stated that he would gladly "suffer the loss of all things" (Philippians 3:8). Why? What could be more enticing than career advancement, the opinions of others, or excellence in one's field? For Paul, his passion is revealed in Philippians 3:10, "that I may know him, and the power of his resurrection, and the fellowship of his sufferings." He was willing to lose all things so that he "may win Christ."

Why have you been given a life? Why have you been born during this time in history? Why do you get married and have kids and make money? Why do you have the talents that you use? Why attend a church, listen to preaching, sing, pray, and serve others? Why share about Jesus? Why enjoy food and drink? Why take a walk in the woods, enjoy the stars in the sky, go to the Grand Canyon? Why play in the snow, or let the rain hit your face, or go to the beach? Why have friendships with people? Why buy a house or go to school or play sports? Why run for public office? Why punish crime, or extend mercy? Why stop sinning? There are hundreds of responses to these inquiries, but there is one common answer that unites them all and a million other questions.

We do all things—eating and drinking, living and dying—to glorify God.

Can you say, as David did, that you ask of God *one thing*, and that the thing *you seek after* is to dwell in His presence? Is your desire with Mary not to be busy with *many things* but to pursue the *one thing* of being in His presence? Is your aim like Paul that you would willingly lose *all things* to hold on to the one thing of knowing Christ? Are all other pursuits garbage in comparison with pursuing Jesus?

Worship means giving "worth" to someone or something in rank, status, or position. Money, relationships, prestige, or any other element or individual that we give worth to, we worship. Everyone worships something, but all are created to worship someone. The Psalmist declared, "Let everything that has breath, praise the Lord" (Psalm 150:6). In the book of Revelation, God on His throne is adored. "Worthy are you our Lord and our God, to receive glory and honor and power" is the ceaseless song (Revelation 4:11). This passage also provides the reason that God is worthy of worship: "for you created all things, and by your will they existed and were created." God alone has "Creator" on His resume, and this quality is why He is worthy of worship. But the verse concludes by informing us that all creation is designed for God's pleasure and by God's will.

The beautiful reality is that the same God who causes the desire to pursue provides the means by which we can know and love Him. This work is a guide that answers the question, "how do we worship God?" Think of these as tools or means to draw closer to Him. This book will categorize these spiritual tools (also known as spiritual disciplines) in four ways: upward, inward, outward, and onward.

The upward elements primarily point heavenward in our relationship with God. The inward elements direct us to other people in the church. The outward elements concentrate on other people in the world. Finally, the onward elements provide us with tools in our continual quest to worship God. Each chapter will provide Scriptural truths demonstrating these characteristics followed by practical tips in applying these disciplines in our lives.

One Christian Reformer famously wrote that the supreme pursuit of Christianity is knowing

God and knowing ourselves.[3] As we pursue God in each of these areas of our life, we will come to know Him intimately. We will soon discover what He thinks, how He feels, why He does what He does. In doing this, we will become like Him, and then discover why we are designed and what our purpose is in this life: to know, love, and glorify Him.

Applying God's Word

1. Read the two following verses:

    "This is eternal life, that they know you, the only true God, and Jesus Christ whom you have sent" (John 17:3).

    "As the deer pants for the water brooks, so my soul longs for you, O God. My soul thirsts for God, for the living God. When will I come and see the face of God?" (Psalm 42:1).

2. How would you describe your spiritual desires?
3. What areas of your life need the most growth, spiritual or otherwise?
4. Pray to praise God for Who He is and what He has done in your life. Ask Him to give you the desire to know, love, and glorify Him.

---

[3] John Calvin, *The Institutes of the Christian Religion*, ed. by John T. McNeill (Westminster Press, 1960), 1:35–39.

1

Upward Spirituality

In music, a "one hit wonder" is a song that achieves success for a short period of time making the artist popular only for that song. In 1990, the Ecuadorian performer Gerardo released his single "Rico Suave." By 1991, the single had charted at #7 on Billboard, and radio listeners were all singing "Rico Suave."[1] By 1992, Gerardo's music would never chart again.

By contrast, a "classic" or "iconic" song is a piece of music that was successful when released and continues to be popular in the modern era. The song never gets stale and becomes attached to the artist. When you think of the artist, you think of

---

[1] https://www.billboard.com/music/gerardo.

the song. Consider Journey's "Don't Stop Believing," or Queen's "We Will Rock You." These are pieces of music that almost everybody has probably heard or sung.

In life we drift toward meaningful experiences: vacation, an adrenaline rush, the reunion with old friends, or the memorable meal. Those special moments last a short time and often cannot be repeated. The Christian life is similar: the time when God spares our life in an accident; when the entire family comes to faith in Christ the first time we share the gospel; or when we feel God's presence closely at a conference. These extraordinary moments cannot be duplicated. They are "one hit wonders."

This chapter is concentrated on the "classics" of spiritual formation. These elements have been used in similar ways by all Christians through history and have never lost their effectiveness. They will still have the force on our lives tomorrow as they did yesterday. They never grow stale, and when one thinks of being a Christian, these characteristics are often what come to mind. We will probably be "singing" these classics when we get to heaven. While there are more, the two spiritual disciplines of Scripture and prayer are iconic to the Christian's life.

Scripture

If you asked me to describe my wife, I might tell you that she is originally from Sicily and studied culinary arts in Paris. She landed a job in St. Petersburg but came to the United States to start her own restaurant. She also tried out for the Sicilian Olympic volleyball team but was injured while skiing in the Swiss Alps. She loves St. Bernard's and NASCAR. Through my sincere tone or sentimental tears, I could convince you that all of this is true. But these descriptions are devoid of reality. I have created a woman from my imagination and passed her off as the real thing. The best way for you to know my wife is to sit down with her and listen to her reveal herself through direct, personal communication. Because the primary way we get to know the truth about someone is through ordinary communicated words.

Voltaire once retorted, "God made man in His own image, then man returned the favor."[2] The Bible reveals who God is through ordinary words,

---

[2] J. M. Wheeler and G. W. Foote, *Voltaire: A Sketch of His Life and Works with Selections from His Writings* (Robert Forder, 1894), 88.

so that we may worship Him properly not in our own image, but in His. God could reveal Himself by writing cryptic notes in clouds, sending an angel to be our friend, or by giving each individual their own special flame to guide them. But his primary means of revelation is through human words. Think of how God could have created the world: the snap of His finger, the tap of His feet, or the twinkle of his eye. He could have thought it all, and it would have happened. Yet all creation came into existence through His words. One of the first actions in the Bible is "He [God] said," which sets the tone throughout the rest of biblical revelation.[3] What God said in His creative decree makes the point more striking: "Let there be...and there was" (Genesis 1; Psalm 33:6, 9).

In Genesis 1, the phrase "God said" is used ten times. In ten words, Genesis 1 sets forth God's law for His creation. In ten words, Exodus 20 sets forth God's law for Israel. When God sought to redeem the world, the call to Abram was simply, "the Lord said." When Israel failed to live accordingly, God spoke in judgments (Isaiah 40:12–31; 42:5–9; Jere-

---

[3] Psalm 33:9; John 1:1-3; 1 Corinthians 8:6; Colossians 1:16; 2 Peter 3:5.

miah 31:35–40). In the fullness of time came Jesus the Word (John 1:1). In the opening pages of his gospel, Mark provided several testimonies presenting Jesus Christ as the Son of God. The first testimony of Jesus' deity was not personal experience or even eyewitness accounts, but "as it is written by Isaiah" and Mark proceeds to provide three passages from the Scriptures to demonstrate this claim (Mark 1:1–3). In the church of Jesus Christ, we have the Word of God proclaimed, explained, and applied to our lives (1 Corinthians 12:27–28).

The importance of reading and hearing the Scriptures has implications for us today. While the Bible does stress the vitality of the proclaimed Word, the Scriptures were written primarily to be heard and read in all of life (Deuteronomy 31:9–13). These sacred words were also written in a context of the community of faith so that reading and hearing the Bible should not just involve ourselves but other believers. The church should be a place where we can share the joy of the Bible together in reading, hearing, praying, singing, and proclaiming. A healthy sermon is an expository sermon where, simply put, the point of the preached message is the point of the text that is read and heard.

Applying God's Word

1. Read through Psalm 119 until you find and write down seven benefits of the Word.
2. God spoke so that we could know Him better. What can you do to better read Scripture as a way to know God?
3. What would be a good time frame each day of the week to come to know God better through His Word?
4. Set a goal to read through the entire Bible. The *Harry Potter* canon is longer than the Bible, you can do it!
5. Ask a pastor or church leader to help you choose a Bible reading plan. You can also search online for "Bible Reading Plan" and find dozens yourself.
6. As an alternative to a structured Bible reading plan, you can begin by reading a chapter in the Gospel of John each day. Then go back and highlight a verse that you can meditate on throughout the day. Each week, you can meet with a friend to read a chapter and discuss it together. After John, you might go to the Psalms and try the same method.

7. Pray that God would give you awe and love for the Bible.

Prayer

Prayer is the natural friend of Bible study. In Bible study, God speaks to us; in prayer we speak to God. Some of the most beautiful prayers in the Scriptures are brief. Moses simply prayed, "Show me your glory" (Exodus 33:18), and he was partially answered. The tax collector prayed, "God be merciful to me the sinner" (Luke 18:13). Jesus said that man went to his house justified. Peter confessed, "Depart from me for I am a sinful man, Lord" (Luke 5:8) but Jesus made him the Rock. At a meeting of the Fellowship of Christian Athletes, Bobby Richardson, former New York Yankee second baseman, offered a prayer that is a classic in brevity and poignancy: "Dear God, Your will, nothing more, nothing less, nothing else."[4]

Thankfully, we have Jesus' disciples asking for us, "Jesus, teach us how to pray." He provided us with "the Lord's prayer," as we call it, which serves

---

[4] Timothy Bowes, *Light Steps: Shedding the Word on Everyday Life* (Xulon Press, 2007), 75.

as for our own prayers. The prayer has two divisions with three petitions and reflects the basics of our Bible study method: God's honor (Matthew 6:9–10) and our need (Matthew 6:11–13). The complete prayer has beautiful connections with our relationship to God as a:

- father/child ("Our Father");
- deity/worshipper ("let your name be holy");
- king/subject ("let your kingdom come");
- master/servant ("let your will be done");
- giver/receiver ("give us this day our daily bread");
- savior/sinner ("forgive us our debts");
- guide/pilgrim ("do not lead us into temptation").

When we pray, we recognize that the God of the Bible is a communicating God. We humble ourselves before Him, the Lord of the universe. Our petitions are framed around a concern for His glory. While we are encouraged to pray for one another, our prayers are not dependent on others. Jesus Christ alone is our High Priest to the Father. Yet there is great value in praying together and for one another in the context of corporate worship. Those prayers often shape or conform our understanding of the Scriptures.

Upward Spirituality

Robert Murray M'Cheyne declared, "what a man is alone on his knees before God, that he is, and no more."[5] If this is true, what kind of person are you? Are you stirred like the disciples to know the importance of prayer in your life? Do you seek to know God more? Do you pray?

Applying God's Word

1. What in your life is currently a higher priority than prayer? Why is prayer a lower priority? What would help you commit to making prayer a higher priority?
2. Why is it difficult for you to pray? What are some current obstacles to prayer in your life?
3. How should the following verses affect your approach to prayer?

    "If you abide in me, and my words abide in you, ask for whatever you wish, and it will be done for you" (John 15:7).

    "You ask and do not receive, because you ask wrongly, in order to spend what you get on your pleasures" (James 4:3).

---

[5] Robert Murray M'Cheyne, as quoted in D.A. Carson, *A Call to Spiritual Reformation: Priorities from Paul and His Prayers* (Baker, 1992), 16.

4. Write these passages on a card or put them on a prompt on your computer or phone so that you can carry through the week with you. Reflect on them often, asking the Spirit to help you understand these statements and to open your mind and heart to how they can enrich the way you pray.
5. Read the story of Peter and John's prayer when they were threatened by Jewish religious rulers (Acts 4:23–31). What can we learn from this example of praying through adversity?
6. Set aside five to ten minutes each day this week to practice listening for God's guidance. Using your Bible, ask God to guide your thoughts and desires toward His word so the Spirit leads you to pray according to the Bible.
7. Record any questions you have from your study of God's word. Allow your study to shape your prayers. For example, if a passage of Scripture emphasizes God's goodness, then let your prayers be guided by that truth.
8. Many people find helpful the ACTS paradigm for praying and certainly this is based on examples we see in Scripture.
    - A–Adoration. Praise flows from our understanding of who God is based on His Word.

Spend some time praising Him for who He is. Use the Bible to do this.
- C–Confession is the admission of our failings before this God who has revealed Himself. God, you are holy, and I am not; you are loving, and I am not; you are powerful, and I am not.
- T–Thanksgiving is praising God for what He has done in our lives: forgiving us, loving us, providing for us.
- S–Supplication is asking God to do what He promised in accordance to His word.

2

Inward Spirituality

My ten-year-old son recalled an event that occurred prior to his afternoon recess. "Dad, you know I held the door for all my class to go outside?" "Really," I replied. "Yeah, I was the last person on the playground because of that and do you know how many said 'thank you'?" "No, I don't, son." "Three, out of seventy-eight students. Only three." I could tell he was in tension over his good deed versus the cost, so I decided to offer my advice. "Well son, Jesus had only one guy out of ten 'thank' Him for healing his disease." My son was in deep thought, and then retorted. "Next time this happens, I think, I'm going to slam the door in their face!"

Part of the "good news" of the Christian message is that when we forget to "thank God" for all the wonderful acts He does for us, He does not "slam the door in our face." Rather He slams sin on His Son so that the door of salvation is held wide open for sinners to enter (2 Corinthians 5:21; Colossians 2:13–15). When one experiences this transformation, the result is not payback but gratitude.

Service

Thankfulness to God is best manifested in service, which is the most regular expression of worship the Bible portrays. The Apostle Peter provided instructions about the importance of service in relationship to worship.

> "As each has received a gift, use it to serve one another, as good stewards of God's varied grace. Whoever speaks, as one who speaks oracles of God; whoever serves, as one who serves by the strength that God supplies, in order that in everything God may be glorified through Jesus Christ. To him belong glory and dominion forever and ever. Amen" (1 Peter 4:10–11).

Twice Peter reminds us that we did not select our gifts; God did. When we serve, we demonstrate that we are "good stewards of God's varied grace." Yet, we do not serve in our own strength, but "by the strength that God supplies." This is why we call them spiritual gifts. A gift is a present; it is something unearned. You did not work for it; you received it. Because they come from God, these gifts are spiritual. When we serve we are using these God-bestowed presents to display what He has done in our lives (Ephesians 2:10).

We worship God rightly when we serve Him faithfully. Jesus said, "No man can serve two masters, for he will either love the one and hate the other, or he will be devoted to the one and despise the other" (Matthew 6:24). Each person has something or someone to whom his or her allegiance is bent. Jesus' point is not the inability to serve; it is the inability to serve two different owners with the same loyalties, the same fervor, the same zeal, and the same affection.

For Jesus, it is not unspiritual to serve two masters; it is impossible to serve two masters. The reason, according to Jesus, is that "you will hate one and love the other; you will be devoted to one and despise the other." You will give preferential treatment to one and not the other; you will cherish one over the other. Because of this, the other will be held in contempt, disinclined, and devalued. Jacob was given two wives from the same father; the oldest was Leah and the youngest was Rachel. Jacob had a deep love for Rachel, but he had to take Leah as part of the package in order to get Rachel (Genesis 29:30–33). Leah and her children always felt like second-class citizens next to Rachel and her children. Why? Because you cannot serve two people equally. You will love the one, and disfavor the other; you will be devoted to the one and despise the other. Service is the best expression of devoted worship to God. If we love Him, we will serve Him and Him alone.

Applying God's Word

1. Read John 13:1–20, concentrating on verse 15. In addition, read Mark 10:45. What do these verses tell you about the value of service?
2. When you think of a servant, what are some characteristics that come to your mind?
3. Read and meditate on Matthew 20:25–28. How do you need to reorient your life to serve others as Jesus did?
4. According to Galatians 5:13, how should we serve one another?
5. Compare a time when you felt pressured to

serve out of obligation and a time when you did it out of relationship. How did you feel in each instance?
6. Look for opportunities to serve others this week.

Giving

In the Bible, serving covers a wide range of actions. Serving can be providing food to others (Luke 10:40; Acts 6:1), instructing people in the Scriptures (Acts 1:17, 25; 21:19), and donating money to the needy (2 Corinthians 8:4; 9:1, 13). In all matters of service, giving is the primary feature. Giving as it involves money is tied to service, which demonstrates where our heart is (Matthew 13:22). "No man can serve two masters . . . you cannot serve God and money." We can be devoted to God. We can be devoted to money. We cannot be devoted to two different masters at the same time. Judas chose his money as his master instead of Jesus, and Paul chose Jesus as his master instead of gain.

In 2 Corinthians 8:8–9, Paul asked the Corinthian church to examine their love for Christ with respect to their giving. "I am testing the sincerity of your love by the diligence of others. For you know the grace of our Lord Jesus Christ, that though He was rich, yet for your sakes He became poor, that you through His poverty might become rich." Paul was testing "the sincerity of their love" by their giving. Love for Christ was to be the reason they brought their money to church for this offering. Remembering what Jesus has done for us motivates that love. "Though He was rich, yet for your sakes He became poor, that you through His poverty might become rich (2 Corinthians 8:9)."

One theologian provided helpful advice when he wrote, "where riches hold the dominion of the heart, God has lost authority."[9] Money is a servant that can greatly benefit the kingdom of God, but money is a terrible master. Many people fail to realize that wealth can possess them. "Greed is idolatry" (Colossians 3:5), and wealth can be our master so that we do its bidding. "Money has enriched his thousands and has damned his tens of thousands."[10]

When Jesus called the rich young ruler to sell all

---

[9] John Calvin, *The Harmony of the Gospels,* trans. by William Pringle and John King (Jazzybee Verlag, n.d.), 1:236.

[10] Attributed to South in Adam Woolever, *Encyclopedia of Quotations: A Treasury of Wisdom, Wit and Humor, Odd Comparisons and Proverbs* (David McKay, 1876), 286.

Inward Spirituality

his possessions and follow him, the man left Jesus in "sorrow because he had great wealth" (Matthew 19:21–23). After committing to follow Jesus, Zacchaeus paid back four times the amount of money he "took" from people as a tax collector and gave half of his possessions to the poor. Jesus replied that "salvation had come to him" (Luke 19:8–9). Money can be a tool used in worship or an idol that we worship. The enemy of our souls, Satan, works on the assumption that every person has a price.

There are three conversions: the conversion of the heart, the conversion of the mind, and the conversion of the purse; the conversion of the purse being the most difficult.[11]

Jesus declared that when we discover what we treasure the most, we will find our hearts (Matthew 6:21). Your perspective on money and possessions may tell you more about your worship than any creed you can recite. Begin to see money not as a "tack on" duty, but as an integral part of worshipping God. This will also adjust our understanding of giving in church worship. God does

---

[11] This statement is often attributed to Martin Luther, yet there is no record of it in his works.

not need our money, yet giving is another humble act of thanksgiving for His redemptive work. By giving, we are expressing that we have already been given a present above and beyond what we deserve. When we are grateful for God's redemptive gift, we will demonstrate generosity with our service and our money.

Applying God's Word

1. If after your death a biographer or your children were to scan your credit card or bank statements for insight into what kind of Christian you were, what would they think? What would be revealed about your walk with Christ?
2. John Wesley posed four questions that will help us decide how to spend money.
   - In spending this money, am I acting as if I owned it, or am I acting as the Lord's trustee?
   - What Scripture requires me to spend this money in this way?
   - Can I offer up this purchase as a sacrifice to the Lord?
   - Will God reward me for this expenditure at the resurrection of the just?

Inward Spirituality

3. A.W. Tozer asked four basic questions:
   - What do we value the most?
   - What would we hate to lose the most?
   - What do our thoughts turn to most frequently when we are free to think of what we will?
   - What affords us the greatest pleasure?
4. Do your answers to these questions reveal that you serve God as your master, or something else?

3

OUTWARD SPIRITUALITY

Many people embrace the satirical mantra, "Christian ministry would be great if it weren't for people." But Christianity involves people, and sometimes people act like what they really are: sinners. Yet the church, like her Lord, is called to go after unhealthy sinners (Mark 2:17). The early church in Jerusalem had a tremendous impact on the world around them, which flowed from a great love for their unsaved neighbors. Today, the church is still called to be the hospital for sin-sick souls. Paul wrote in 1 Corinthians 13:2, "if I have the gift of prophecy, and know all mysteries and all knowledge; and if I have all faith, so as to remove mountains, but do not have love, I am nothing." The Bible presents two consistent ways that believers can demonstrate the gospel to a lost world: conduct and conversation.

We love unbelievers by how we behave

Do good to others

"In the same way, let your light shine before others, so that they may see your good works and give glory to your Father who is in heaven" (Matthew 5:16). The ultimate purpose of doing good to unbelievers is not that they would be impressed by our morality, but that good works would bring attention to God, the source of all good.

Stop complaining

"Do all things without grumbling or disputing, that you may be blameless and innocent, children of God without blemish in the midst of a crooked and twisted generation, among whom you shine as lights in the world" (Philippians 2:14–15). One of the ways we "shine as lights in the world" is by not complaining against our Christian family. Griping about the people of God and praise of the

God of His people cannot coexist. Paul argued that a complaining Christian undermines the gospel of peace he professes. Why would someone be convinced to come to Jesus, the Prince of Peace, if His followers were "Debbie Downers," "Norman Negatives," and anything but peaceable?

Live decently and labor faithfully

"Aspire to live quietly, and to mind your own affairs, and to work with your hands, as we instructed you, so that *you* may walk properly before outsiders and be dependent on no one" (1 Thessalonians 5:11–12). A problem that was threatening the unity of the church in Thessalonica was that some Christians were neglecting work, staying home, gossiping, and living off the labor of others. Paul spotted a spreading danger; this "dependency culture" in the church may affect believer's witness to unbelievers in their community. The best advice for reaching the lost? Get a job and mind your own business.

Be holy

"But you are a chosen race, a royal priesthood, a

holy nation, a people for his own possession, that you may proclaim the excellencies of him who called you out of darkness into his marvelous light. Once you were not a people, but now you are God's people; once you had not received mercy, but now you have received mercy. Beloved, I urge you as sojourners and exiles to abstain from the passions of the flesh, which wage war against your soul. Keep your conduct among the Gentiles honorable, so that when they speak against you as evildoers, they may see your good deeds and glorify God on the day of visitation" (1 Peter 2:9–12).

A pastor preached at a prison. Afterwards, one of the inmates approached him and said, "That was really great. I'm glad to see a brother in Christ. You know, I'm in the Lord's work too." He told the pastor the name of a Christian organization he worked for. Somewhat puzzled, the pastor asked what he was doing in jail, "Oh, I got several traffic tickets, and I never paid them off, so I was sentenced to 90 days in jail." The pastor said to him, "Do the rest of us a favor, and don't tell anybody you are a Christian. We don't need that kind of negative publicity." You may not be in prison, but there are other ways that your lifestyle can undermine your testimony. Never are we more like

Christ than when we are most unlike the unbelieving world. If a sinner were to spend one day with you, at the end of that day, would they know what Jesus looked like?

Love other believers

Jesus said "the world will know you are my disciples if you love one another" (John 13:35). Not only is love a supreme sign that you follow Jesus, but love for one another is a convincing proof to an unloving world. It is curious that Jesus did not say to love unbelievers here, but that love for other believers will persuade the world of authentic Christianity.

Do not needlessly offend

"Give no offense to Jews or to Greeks or to the church of God, just as I try to please everyone in everything I do, not seeking my own advantage, but that of many, that they may be saved" (1 Corinthians 10:32–33). No amount of personal freedom is worth gospel ministry to others. The message of the gospel will offend unbelievers; let us make sure our personal preferences do not.

We love unbelievers by what we say

In the task of presenting the gospel to others, some Christians are like an Arctic River; frozen over at the mouth. While the Bible emphasizes the content of the gospel, it also stresses the manner by which the gospel is to be proclaimed.

Be wise and gracious

"Walk in wisdom toward outsiders, making the best use of the time. Let your speech always be gracious, seasoned with salt, so you may know how you ought to answer each person" (Colossians 4:5–6).

A wise believer knows when to speak and when to shut up. In the gospels, Jesus transformed people by mercy, not by brute force. Let us make sure that the message of the gospel is cutting the conscience, not our own tongues.

Be ready, gentle, and respectful

"If you should suffer for righteousness' sake, you will be blessed. Have no fear of them, nor be troubled, but in your hearts honor Christ the Lord as holy, always being prepared to make a defense to anyone who asks you for a reason for the hope that is in you; yet do it with gentleness and respect, having a good conscience, so that when you are slandered, those who revile your good behavior in Christ may be put to shame. For it is better to suffer for doing good, if that should be God's will, than for doing evil" (1 Peter 3:14–16).

Unbelievers will react to the gospel message and sometimes their reaction is not always positive. In fact, it may be quite personal. When those slanderous times come, the believer is not called to be a doormat, but to be a bulldog—a bulldog tenacious with gentleness and respect. Jesus' words to his disciples ring true: "be wise as serpents and innocent as doves" (Matthew 10:16).

Applying God's Word

1. Read 1 Corinthians 15:3–5 for a good summary of the gospel.
2. Make a list of three to five people with whom you can share the gospel. What might be a scenario for each person that would allow you to share the gospel with them?
3. Pray to ask God to provide you with boldness to open your mouth and speak the gospel.

4

―――――――

Onward Spirituality

Now that we have considered basic components of upward, inward, and outward spirituality, where do we go from here? In this chapter, we will consider an array of questions to help you practice these essential disciplines consistently. These are meant not to be exhaustive, but rather to begin the process of helping you implement your own spiritual disciplines. These applications are divided into three parts (personal, family, and community) to remind us that glorifying God is all of life. You might consider discussing one part per meeting with a mentor or leader.

Upward

Personal

1. Is your spiritual life satisfying? Why or why not?
2. Do you trust in Jesus for the forgiveness of your sins and the salvation of your soul? Are you willing to believe and obey Him?
3. Are you willing to make the Bible the ultimate authority in your life?
4. From your weekly readings of the Bible, select and consider one verse throughout the week. Ask God to reveal the truth of that verse so that you can apply it as a regular part of your life.
5. What frustrations do you regularly encounter in Bible study and prayer, and how may you resolve those difficulties?
6. Are your prayers consistent with what you are reading from the Bible? Consider the content of the word that you are reading and conform your prayers to those passages.
7. Is there a time of the day and a place that works best for consistent Bible reading and prayer in your life?
8. What do you enjoy most about your Bible study and prayer life?

9. What has your Bible study and prayer life been teaching you about God?

Family

1. Are you and your spouse growing spiritually, or are there tensions? In what ways?
2. Are your kids believers? In what ways can you continually point them to Jesus?
3. Do your kids love God because they see His love in you?
4. What does your family need to learn the most about God and how can you help them?
5. How can you cultivate a place of Bible study and prayer in the home?
6. What can you pray about for your family and with your family?
7. Are there any ways that you and your family can better prepare for Sunday worship?
8. Use a hymnal in family worship or sing sacred songs together in the home.

Community

1. What has your Bible study and prayer life been teaching you about your relationships?

2. Are you a part of a church where true worship of God exists?
3. In choosing a church, pay attention to how often people talk about God, and what they say about Him.
4. In choosing a church, listen to elements in the worship service and see if those elements speak of God clearly and accurately, or speak about man regularly (music that is sung, the prayers that are prayed, promotion of ministry, preaching, etc.).
5. In choosing a church, read as much of the church's literature as possible: confession of faith, vision statements, Bible study material, children's material, gospel tracts, etc. This will give you glimpse at whether the church has a good grasp of God and what they emphasize the most.
6. In choosing a church, look for how the church prioritizes and talks about church matters. For example, is there a concern for the spiritual health of the congregation, or a concentrated emphasis on numbers?
7. In choosing a church, be careful if there is too much talk or emphasis on 'we' and not 'Him.' For example, does the church endlessly talk

about programs or about the person and work of Jesus? Or "look what we did" rather than "look who He is." In such churches, God is probably being used as a means to an end.

8. In choosing a church, look for an emphasis on the Bible. Is the Word central to the worship service or at the periphery? A sign of a healthy church is that in corporate worship they pray the Word, read the Word, sing the Word, and speak the Word.

9. In choosing a church, observe whether people bring and use their Bibles.

10. In choosing a church, avoid a church where the pastor consistently reads the text of Scripture and departs from it never to return again. In such cases, the Bible is a launching pad for his sermon. If you attend a church like this long enough, you will never grow beyond what the preacher thinks about an issue.

11. In choosing a church, ponder the time spent on the preaching of the Word in comparison to other things. For example, if a church sings for 45 minutes but listens to preaching for 15 minutes, the chances are that the Word of God is not a top priority.

12. In choosing a church, consider whether you

see the people applying the Word of God in their daily lives.

13. In choosing a church, consider whether they discuss the Word or the personality and style of the preacher. Are you wowed by the stories or wooed by the Word?

14. In choosing a church, consider whether the church is structured by Scripture or by tradition or expediency.

15. In choosing a church, consider whether decisions are made based on truth or on popularity or expediency.

16. In choosing a church, consider whether there is an emphasis on biblical theology, or on what works pragmatically.

17. In choosing a church, consider whether the church measures success by numerical results, or by faithfulness to God's Word.

18. In what areas of your life is your church providing you with the most growth?

19. What keeps you from consistently praying for others?

20. How can you help your church pray for one another more effectively?

21. Do you have anyone in your life that will consistently pray with you and for you?

22. What needs in your church can you pray for now?

INWARD

Personal

1. In your life, are there areas of service that are driven by moralism or self-righteousness?
2. In your weekly Bible reading, what do your passages teach about service and stewardship?
3. Pray and look for opportunities to serve others. Ask your pastor how you can serve him or others in the church.
4. Are you willing to advance the gospel by giving your money generously to the church?
5. Think of ways that giving money is connected to worship.

Family

1. Are there any ways in which you are giving your family a negative view of the church?
2. How can you prepare your family for Sunday worship with the church?

3. How can you foster an atmosphere of service in your family?
4. How can you teach your kids about giving?

Community

1. What are some reasons people give for leaving a church? How do these reasons line up with Scripture? Do these reasons say anything about love for the church?
2. How does church membership clarify the differences between believers and unbelievers?
3. What may a person's unwillingness to serve in the church indicate?
4. In what ways does church membership advance the gospel?
5. With a Bible and a Bible word search, find all verses with the phrase "one another" and see how they describe church body life.
6. How could your church create an atmosphere of servants?
7. What do you love to do that you could use to serve others in the church?
8. If you could be involved in serving in any ministry what would it be?
9. Who can you call, text, e-mail, or send a card

to in order to encourage?
10. Who can you invite over for a meal with the purpose of encouraging them?
11. Are there new people in your church to whom you can reach out and make them welcome?
12. Have you asked your pastors in what areas of the church you can serve?
13. Is there a friendship with someone at the church you can invest in to promote growth in your lives?
14. Would your church discipline you if you continued in open, unrepentant sin?
15. Is the church you attend a place you would want your children to grow up in order to know who Jesus is and how to live like Him?
16. Is this fellowship a place of confrontation, confession, forgiveness, and repentance or a place of backbiting, gossip, bitterness, and friction?
17. Are the elders/pastors men of integrity or is there regular inconsistency in their life and their profession?
18. Is there joyful submission to pastors on the part of the congregation, or disheartened division?
19. Are the church's leaders actively serving the needs of the congregation, or are they a 'good ole boy' fraternity?

20. Are the members active in giving money and serving with joy, or is it a few carrying the load?

Outward

Personal

1. Who can you share the gospel with?
2. Who can you invite over for a meal in order to get to know them for the gospel's sake?
3. What missionary or missions project can you pray for?
4. Who can you ask to attend worship with you?
5. How can you minister the gospel in your neighborhood, school, or job?
6. Are there any aspects of evangelism that cause you fear? What can you do to learn from those fears?

Family

1. Do you live in such a way that your family recognizes who Jesus is?
2. Do your children and spouse know Jesus?

3. Are there any aspects of the gospel your family are confused by?
4. How can your family pray for the lost?
5. How can your family pray for missions?

Community

1. In your church, is the gospel of grace clearly on display, or is it confused by works righteousness?
2. In your church, do members illustrate an understanding of the gospel, conversion, and evangelism?
3. In your church, do the people talk much and pray for the conversion of others?
4. Does your church focus on decisions or on genuine conversion?
5. Does your church's evangelism strategy emphasize faithfulness to the gospel, or is it more like a marketing strategy?
6. Does your church's evangelism method emphasize God performing the work, or is it emotionally manipulative?

Conclusion

When I began pastoral ministry, I led a weekly Bible study in a nursing home. Many of these saints were industrious, hard-working people in their younger years, but when I knew them, they could barely move or speak. When they did speak, their words were often incoherent. Many in the group had families, but they couldn't name their own son or daughter. On one particular visit, I was running late and running on empty in my ministry tank. As I walked in the door, feelings of self-pity and fatigue overwhelmed me. I did not have anything to offer this group.

Then I heard an out of tune piano played by a resident that was often off key and tone deaf, but on this day, I heard the voices of 40 residents that rivaled any earthly anthem I have heard. I stood outside the room listening to the cracked voices but pure hearts of tired old saints singing 'Then with my waking thoughts, bright with Your praise, out of my stony griefs, Bethel I'll raise; so, by my woes to be nearer my God to thee, Nearer my God to Thee, Nearer to Thee.' I know many Christians who can sing but have lost their song. The saints in that nursery home taught me the reverse.

Redemptive history is moving toward that great drama when all heaven sings, "Worthy are you ... for you were slain, and by your blood you ransomed people for God from every tribe and language and people and nation" (Revelation 5:9). This heavenly drama demonstrates that the reality of eternity is worshipping God: being taught by Him, talking to Him, serving Him, presenting our gifts to Him, and testifying of His redemption. To love, know and enjoy Him is the *one thing* worth pursuing now and forever.

NOTES

Notes

NOTES

Notes

NOTES

www.ingramcontent.com/pod-product-compliance
Lightning Source LLC
Chambersburg PA
CBHW052104110526
44591CB00013B/2350